ISBN No.   978-1-905546-48-0

Printed & Bound by Pen2print, Ferrybridge, WF11 8PL
www.pen2print   Tel: 01977 678371

About The Authors

Eddie and Judy Colquhoun live in Ferrybridge (West Yorkshire), and both work full time in the caring profession. They love life, have two grown up children and one grandchild, and have a burning desire to help everyone into a more fulfilling life! They are part of the leadership of Hope City Church in Leeds and put a practical spin on all they say and do.

Eddie and Judy have written a very practical book about a very under involved stage of life - midlife! If you dare to read it, it could help you avoid the dreaded 'midlife crisis' and so go on to your God given future! If it's too late, and you've 'been there and done that', this book will give you hope and an action plan for reinventing your life and emerging out of the midlife storms with renewed vigour and vitality!

Eddie and Judy know what it's like to chart a course through storms, doldrums, high seas and heavy winds of life! They have learnt how to navigate the stages of life successfully and have found themselves in their best season yet through applying the principles and advice given in this book in the early part of their own lives. May this book be to you a navigator that charts a course through your current life stage into a new and exciting season that fills you with a sense of purpose and passion and an overwhelming feeling that all of the best bits in life had been left to right now!

Dave Gilpin
Senior Pastor
Hope City Church

Eddie & Judy Colquhoun

Acknowledgements

To Pastor Dave Gilpin (Senior Pastor of Hope City Church) for inspiring both of us to recognise 'everyone has a book in them'. To Pastors Chris and Gosia Denham of Hope City Church Leeds, our good friends who have encouraged us along the way. Also to Dave Gilpin and Gosia Denham for editing our book (they must have been very patient with us - thank you). To all our colleagues, in both our work places, for being interested in what we had to say about 'how to do midlife well'. To Tammy, a wonderful admin assistant who brilliantly formatted the book and prepared it for publishing (thank you, Tammy, you're a star!) To all our family for being so supportive, and particularly our son, Jonny, for his technical 'know how' on the computer. To God for being a loving Father, encouraging us, saving us, keeping us, making our marriage wonderful, and giving us the life and determination to write this book.

Eddie and Judy Colquhoun

Contents

Foreword

By Judy

Life seemed to be fairly normal. We were both in our early 50's with two healthy children now grown up and making their own way in life. We were both in interesting and challenging careers, both involved in training and taking further qualifications. For thirty years we had been involved in local Church life. Eddie was involved with music and pastoral care in the Church and I had been involved in children's work and organising events in the Church. We had been a part of pioneering a fresh new congregation which began with great expectation, but, ten years on, a supermarket chain wanted to buy the building we were in and a decision was made to bring the two congregations back together again. We didn't understand what was happening but it became clear that the direction the Church was heading in was not the direction that we felt God had called us to. We were left with no other option but to make a huge and momentously painful decision to leave. Struggling with pain and disappointment we had no idea where we would go it seemed a good idea to us to just visit churches for the next year, sit at the back and not get involved. God must really have been laughing at us. I could imagine him saying, *'Oh Yeah, that's what you think'*. Through a chance visit to Hillsong in London we were signposted to Hope City Church and that's where the mid life adventure began. Our experience opened our eyes to how important our midlife actions really are and how the decisions and actions that we take can have huge relationship with the rest of our lives.

There has been a momentous change in our life and attitudes and we are so grateful to God for bringing us into a place of abundance, and into a new season of growth, prosperity, and seeing his faithfulness.

We were not aware of any books that have looked at the mid life stage of life and the issues that every mid-lifer faces. Don't worry, it's not a book about menopausal women, or preparing for retirement. It is a book about living life to the full no matter what age you are. There is a great truth in the word of God that has become so precious to us, particularly in our mid-life, that He doesn't want us to be mediocre, beige, or just 'get by' in our attitude and lifestyle, but he wants us to have life and to live it to its absolute limit.

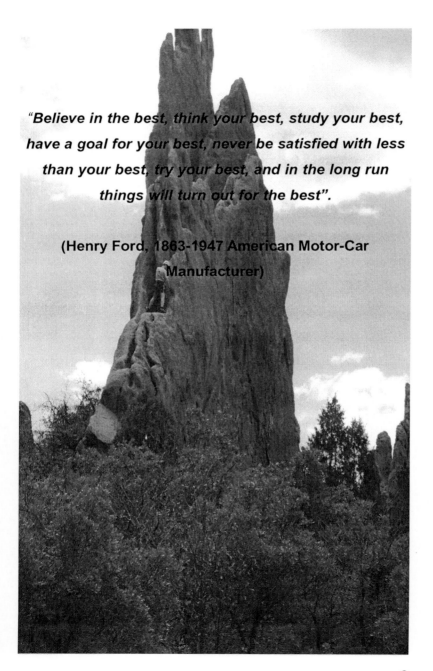

"Believe in the best, think your best, study your best, have a goal for your best, never be satisfied with less than your best, try your best, and in the long run things will turn out for the best".

(Henry Ford, 1863-1947 American Motor-Car Manufacturer)

Chapter 1

Stop! Don't Have a Mid-Life Crisis

Have a Mid-life Adventure!

(Eddie and Judy)

So what is midlife? It is defined as the years between 40 and 60. Midlife is an area that has received very little attention from students of human development, who have tended to concentrate on childhood, adolescence, or old age. There are therefore many myths and falsehoods about midlife.

People experiencing midlife now are part of the "baby boom" generation. Baby boomers were reared with a strong sense of entitlement and enormous expectations that the future would always be better. They were freed at an early age to focus on themselves – on individuality, personal fulfilment and instant gratification. Defined by unprecedented economic prosperity and rock n roll, the me generation broke through previous taboos on divorce, sex and self fulfilment.

Today's mid-lifers are facing many changes. They are concerned about growing old in a society obsessed with youth and beauty.

Why is it that couples who has lived a happy married life suddenly after 20 or so years of marriage become discontented with their lot to the extent that they start to look outside their marriage to find themselves again? Mid life causes many people to believe that the grass is greener on the other side. A younger woman or man showing an interest can be flattering to a mid-lifer who feels they are not as attractive as they used to be. This attraction can often grow and develop into a full blown affair. Mid lifers often feel life is a rut, and everything is same old same old. Very often mid lifers live with regrets if only they had done this or that, how quickly life has flown by and now there are younger, better looking and more technically able people ready to take over. Anything that makes the mid lifer feel young, attractive and worth while can be a temptation. There is as much need to be careful of your relationships in mid life as there is when you are a teenager!

Mid-lifers are caught in the middle between still having responsibilities for supporting children, whilst also having added responsibility for elderly parents.
Do you view the future as a time of descent and decline? Well there is good news! Mid-life does not have to be the beginning of the end, but rather a new beginning and a new platform for growth and opportunity.

Here are just some of the people who achieved their greatest success at midlife!

Colonel Harland Sanders – pioneer of Kentucky Fried Chicken

In 1930 Sanders then 40 years old was operating a service station in Kentucky. He began cooking for hungry travellers who stopped for petrol. He invented several regional dishes and began to sell them as complete meals to busy time-strapped families.

Within four years, his establishment was listed in Duncan Hines *"Adventures in Good Eating".* As more people started coming strictly for the food, he moved across the street to increase his capacity. Over the next ten years, he perfected his secret blend of 11 herbs and spices and the basic cooking technique that is still used today.

In 1955, confident of the quality of his fried chicken, the Colonel devoted himself to developing his chicken franchising business. Less than 10 years later, Sanders had more than 600 KFC franchises in the U.S. and Canada, and in 1964 he sold his interest in the U.S. Company for $2 million to a group of investors. Today the restaurant company is the world's largest in terms of system units with nearly 32,500 in more than 100 countries and territories.

Until he was fatally stricken with leukaemia in 1980, at the age of 90, the Colonel travelled 250,000 miles a year visiting KFC restaurants around the world!

Dame Anita Roddick – Founder of the Body Shop

Anita Roddick was the founder of the Body Shop chain which now operates world wide.

Today the Body Shop chain operates in 34 countries and has over 500 shops.

In 1984 Anita Roddick brought her company to the Stock Exchange. Her brilliantly simple initial idea has grown into a concern with an annual turn over of £60 million.

In her midlife Dame Anita became involved in many projects that affected for good the lives of many people. In 1990, aged 48 she set up a project to refurbish 3 Romanian orphanages, and the work extended into Albania and Bosnia. In 2000 she was involved in the 'Body Shop Human Rights Award where $300,000 was awarded to selected grassroots groups fighting for human rights globally. In 2003 she was involved in 'Help stop violence in the home'-a domestic violence campaign with Refuge (the UK's largest single provider of accommodation and support to women and children experiencing domestic violence). In the same year Anita was awarded the Order of the British Empire for her outstanding work.

Ricky Tomlinson – Actor

Born in 1939 in Liverpool, he spent his childhood playing among the bombed and destroyed houses from the Second World War. After leaving school he became a plasterer but spent all his spare time playing in the local clubs with various bands and comedy sketch teams. Following many difficult years, including a stint in prison for an offence he still refutes, he became an actor in his forties and became a household name for his role as Jim Royale in the hit series 'The Royale Family'

William & Catherine Booth – Founders of the Salvation Army

William and Catherine Booth the founders of the Salvation Army were born in Nottingham in the early 1800's. William Booth was no stranger to poverty being only 14 when his father died and already working as a pawn brokers apprentice to supplement the family income and completing a six year apprenticeship. It was in those early years he developed a great hatred for poverty and suffering which he saw on a day to day basis.

At the age of 65 along with his wife Catherine the work of the Christian Mission began which later became the Salvation Army. William preached to the poor and the ragged and Catherine spoke to the wealthy gathering support for their financially demanding work.

Smith Wigglesworth

Smith Wigglesworth was born in 1859 and at the age of seven he was working twelve hours a day with his father to supplement the family finances. As a result he had little education.

Smith and his wife Polly made a pledge to God that they would have no medicine, no doctors, or drugs of any kind in their home.

Smith Wigglesworth was gripped by a violent pain and was brought home. He and Polly prayed all night but as he got worse, he thought it was his *"home call"*. They had agreed that if either of them thought it was their "home call" the other would send for the doctor to avoid the embarrassment of an inquest and the condemnation of outsiders. The doctor diagnosed Smith Wigglesworth with appendicitis in an advanced state. The only hope was an immediate operation which Smith refused. An elderly lady and young man came and prayed for him. Smith went downstairs and told his surprised wife "I am healed". He went on to preach the gospel in many parts of the world for another 40 years. He was instrumental in bringing thousands of people to salvation, baptism in the Spirit and healing in God. About twenty people were raised from the dead during Smith Wigglesworth's ministry.

In 1907, at the age of 48, he was baptised in the Holy Spirit and spoke in other tongues. This experience enabled this unschooled man to preach eloquent and life changing messages all over England and world wide. He believed his sermons should make his hearers either glad or mad. He would say, "If you do not progress every day, you are backsliding".
In 1937 Smith Wigglesworth marched into the office of the secretary of the Apostolic Faith Mission and prophesied what we now know as the Charismatic Revival. Smith Wigglesworth also had an international ministry, well into his 'midlife', and ministered in the US, Australia, New Zealand, South Africa, The Pacific Island, India, Ceylon, and several countries in Europe. Wigglesworth is considered one of the most influential

evangelists in the early history of Pentecostalism and is also credited with helping give the movement a large religious audience.

Winston Churchill

Perhaps one of the greatest and visionary leaders of all time was Sir Winston Leonard Spencer Churchill born in 1874. He became a British politician and prime minister in 1940 – 1945 and 1951 – 1955. He was widely regarded as Britain's greatest century statement and was celebrated for his national leadership during World War II. Churchill was undoubtedly an inspirational wartime leader. His pugnacity and rousing speeches rallied the nation to continue to fight. He is particularly remembered for his courageous stand as prime minister in 1940 and 1941 when Britain stood alone against perhaps the most dangerous adversary it had faced in its long history.

In the Daily Express newspaper we once read an article entitled " No Mid-Life Crisis for the Adventure Generation", which, in so many ways, puts into words what we believe, and are passionate about. The article quoted from a report written by the 'Future Laboratory', saying that *"the image of the stereotypical middle-aged worker as down trodden and tied down as they plod their way slowly towards retirement has undergone a huge transformation".* They are then described as *'uniquely confident'*, and with an independent attitude to life. Instead of suffering a mid-life crisis, today's 45 to 55 year olds have been dubbed the 'Generation Liberati'. They are experiencing a "mid-life release energetic" that is enabling them to change their job, home and outlook on life. They are open-minded, independent and confident, growing old no longer means fading away.

Here are ten P's to having a positive attitude to midlife

1. **Passion** – What are the things that you are passionate about? What gets you up in a morning? Stop playing safe, doing your duty and start to enjoy what you do and pursue the path of passion.

2. **Purpose** – in the Bible Queen Esther, in a very difficult time of Jewish history, was called to save the nation. Her Uncle, Mordecai, told her she was "born for such a time as this". We also need to believe that we are destined for a purpose and that we can carry on fulfilling that purpose until we take our last breath. There is no better way than knowing in your heart that you are following your purpose and living the life you are meant to live.

3. **Power** – Power involves developing the unwavering confidence or belief in yourself, that you can accomplish your purpose. We have found that a great source of power for us comes from our deep faith in God.

4. **Planning** – It is so easy to become an aimless drifter in midlife. So take action think about the things you want to do, the places you want to visit, the qualification you want to achieve, when you want to retire, and start to plan. Then keep reviewing your progress: how are you doing; are you on track; if not, why not. Sometimes life throws things at us that steer us off course, but we do not have to stay that way - we can apply our planning compass and get our life back on track.

5. **Perspective** – Have you ever looked at the famous drawing where some people see an old hag and others can see a beautiful lady?

Both things are there - it depends what your perspective is, thus, in life, you can have the half- empty glass approach or you can choose to have a positive attitude to life.

The world is becoming a smaller place, with overseas travel now common place. It is not out of the ordinary for 'working people'to travel to exotic places, go on safaris, cruises, places that our parents only dreamt of visiting, or read about in books. Didn't someone once say "the world is your oyster"? Well, they weren't wrong! All you need to do is go out there, **take the first step!**

6. **Positivity** – Are you someone people want to be around? Is your enthusiasm contagious? Do you lighten other people's spirits? Are you generous with praise and encouragement? Do you see the glass half- full rather than half -empty?

7. **Productiveness** – Be a producer. God has created us to be over comers, to produce wealth, not just to live for ourselves, but to bring increase from our lives and to live for God.

8**. Preparation** – Being prepared is not just a motto for the Scout Movement. We should always be prepared to give an account of what our purpose in life is.

9. **Playfulness** – Don't ever stop having a playful spirit. Do things for fun, laugh a lot. Don't be so dignified that you can't enjoy your self.

Remember, even King David was prepared to be undignified as he celebrated by dancing with all his might when the Ark of the Covenant came back to Jerusalem. (NIV Bible 11 Samuel chapter 6 v 14)

10. **Perseverance** – Remember, life is a marathon not a sprint race. You have to be prepared to persevere. Keep your eye on your dream and goal and never get to the end of your life with only a heap of regrets.

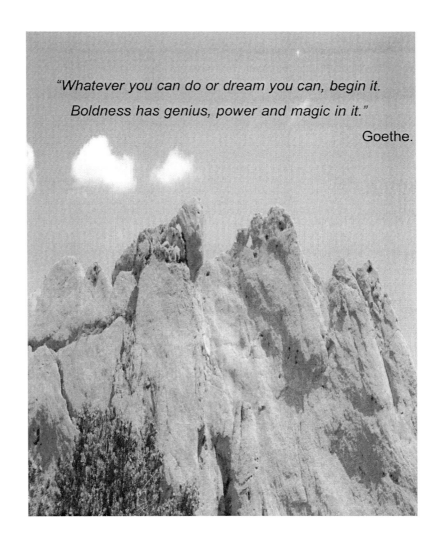

"Whatever you can do or dream you can, begin it.
Boldness has genius, power and magic in it."

Goethe.

Chapter 2

God Doesn't Want Saga Christians

50's Are The New 30's!

(Judy)

I was about to hit one of those milestone birthday moments the big 50. What did the postman bring? Birthday cards and a dustbin full of offers from Saga now that I had reached this distinguished age. How do they know? Who told them I was 50? Why do all the photographs in their literature show people in their seventies rather than fun- loving, funky -dressing people like me?

So what does God say about the 40+ generation? The Bible says in Psalm 1:

"*Blessed is the man who does not walk in the counsel of the wicked or stand in the way of sinners or sit in the seat of mockers. But his delight is in the law of the Lord and on his law he meditates day and night. He is like a tree planted by streams of water which yields its fruit in season and whose leaf does not wither.*"

I have determined that I do not want to be a tree with withered leaves. I want to be fresh and bring refreshment to others.

One of the places that I had always wanted to visit was Pompeii. So that was my 50th birthday treat - four wonderful days in Naples. I wasn't disappointed, Pompeii was spectacular, and demonstrated how ingenious the Romans were and how many of today's items come from those times. In addition we had a trip on the Amalfi coast and a day in Capri. I have stored all those pictures of the beautiful sights we saw in my memory banks.

Eddie and I have a list of places that we would like to visit and we are gradually working our way through them. It is good to have dreams in all different aspects of our life and then work towards achieving them. Too many people procrastinate and find excuses about not being able to fulfil their dreams. Others stop dreaming altogether and slip slowly into old age.

Dreaming is good for the soul, mind and body. Dreaming expands your horizons, causes you to be inspirational and keeps you continually looking for bigger and better things.

Here are ten ways dreaming helps to keep you inspirational.

1. Dreaming can motivate the small gift within you to become a great talent. When David Beckham was kicking the ball around as a boy, dreaming about being a professional footballer motivated him to hone his skills, practice and be ultra- fit. That dream has eventually led him to become one of the most famous footballers of our time. How many other people do you know start with a dream which becomes their reality?

2. Don't compare yourself to other people. Don't copy other people's dreams - you need your own. You are unique and special. There is no other person like you. You might be the only person (like Esther) who can change a situation.

3. Never, give up. Don't be disappointed if things do not happen straight away or go to plan. Look how long it took for Joseph to see his dreams come to pass. But he never gave up even when it looked as if it was impossible for his dreams to ever come to pass.

4. Watch people do not steal your dreams. There is a big difference in culture between Britain and the United States

of America. Unfortunately in Britain there is a culture of cynicism, pulling people down, looking for the faults in people rather than the potential. In America their culture promotes dreaming and aspiration. Children are taught that nothing is outside their scope or possibility. So make sure you spend time with people who will encourage you and your dreams and aspirations.

5. Every new thing starts with someone's dream. Every new invention, new computer program, new painting or sculpture, piece of music or dance start with someone having a creative thought.

6. Dreaming stops you becoming mundane and ordinary. The Bible tells us that we were made to be people of vision. Amplified Bible Proverbs 29 v 18 "*Where there is no vision people perish.*"

7. Grasp the opportunities to see your dreams fulfilled. On the very first series of 'Britain's Got Talent', an unknown mobile telephone salesman suddenly had the opportunity to fulfil his dream and show the nation his beautiful operatic voice. We would never have heard of Paul Potts if he had stayed at home and not gone to the audition.

8. If you know that you have a gift, or talent, then make sure that you are using it. Then look for opportunities to expand and extend your gift or talent. Remember we all have at least one gift or talent, so there is no excuse - start using it now and look where that can take you.

9. Do something about your dream: if you want to be a musician then you need to learn an instrument; if you want to be a long distant runner then you need to start to train; if you want to be slim then you need to start a programme; if you want to be a leader hang around other good leaders.

10. You have a choice - choose not to settle for second best. Inside you there is so much potential. Choose to let God develop your character and skills. Maybe you could be the next Picasso, Bruce Springstein, David Beckham, or MP for the city you live in. It begins with a choice.

11. And here's one more for the road. It's never too late. You are never too old to dream.

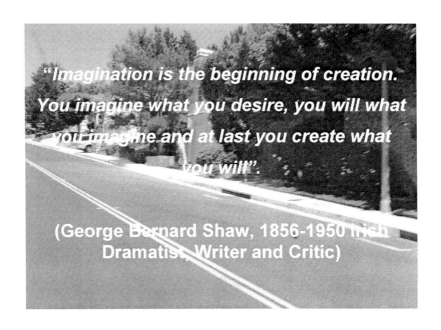

"*Imagination is the beginning of creation. You imagine what you desire, you will what you imagine and at last you create what you will*".

(George Bernard Shaw, 1856-1950 Irish Dramatist, Writer and Critic)

Chapter 3

If You Don't Know Where You're Going,

Any Road Will Take You There!

(Eddie)

Just in case you didn't know, this was the title of one of the last songs George Harrison wrote before he died of cancer in 2001, and it seemed to me a good title for a chapter of a book concerning where we are all heading in life. These days, when we set off on a car journey, we have maps, route planners, and even satellite navigation to guide us, talk to us, and get us on to the right road.

So why is it that, in other areas of our lives, we simply settle for where we have always gone, do the things we've always done, instead of planning our route and seeking guidance from people who are actually living in the direction of where we really wish to go.

In most areas of our working lives we produce, action plans, objectives, work schedules, service level agreements, and policies on every conceivable subject you can imagine. So why do some of us find ourselves simply drifting along, without any thought of taking stock of our position or evaluating how we are achieving our objectives?

One summer we had a great holiday in Florida enjoying the Disney World parks. At the end of the holiday we were returning the hire care to the depot, which happened to be very near the airport. Because of this, we ran the car's petrol down to almost empty. As we approached the car hire depot I missed the turning, and simply took the next turning off to the right- big mistake! The next thing we knew we were on the freeway heading out of Florida. There were at least three toll booths to go through and we had virtually no American money left for the booths. At moments like these you really should pray, but we all panicked especially Judy, who exclaimed rather loudly, *"reverse down the motorway"*. I tried to remain calm and hold the situation together, by asking for a mint, which I felt would help me think straight. Judy continued to say *"reverse down the motorway"*.

We don't make the best decisions in our lives, when we panic, go it alone, or refuse to take good advice! At the next exit on the freeway we were able to pull off and asked advice at the next garage. Although we thought we had been travelling for hours and were miles away we actually were five minutes from the care hire depot. We got back on track and I got my mint!

So how do we find direction for our lives? At the age of 16, the mines in Scotland began to close and my family relocated to Knottingley to work in the newly opened Kellingley Coal Mine. For eight years I worked as a mechanical fitter, but it was not something that I wanted to do for the rest of my life. Direction came into my life in the form of a friend who suggested to me that I could do something different than work down the pit all my life. In my case it certainly changed the direction of my life, and for the better. To enable me to obtain some qualifications I changed jobs to work in the Water Board on days rather than shifts, so that I could go to evening school. I spent the next two years at evening school and eventually gained five O levels. I then started to apply for positions that involved working with people, and eventually was successful in gaining a position as an Education Welfare Officer in the City of Leeds. From those early days,I went on to train as a social worker, a clinical and pastoral counsellor, and to have a very successful career helping young people gain the maximum benefit from their education, whilst moving into more leadership roles and all because I listened to advice about direction for my life!

Herbert Harrison, a preacher I once heard, gave a great analogy about how to be wise in finding direction for our lives. He said when a boat comes into harbour it lines up the lights to ensure that there is a safe path into the harbour. He referred to it as "lining up the lights". This principle can be used in our lives. We should never just respond to a feeling to move, change jobs or other major changes in our lives without ensuring the lights are lined up. The lights we use are good counsel, wise words, good instruction and the Word of God.

Here are some wise words from the book of Proverbs in the Bible regarding direction for areas of our lives.

- *"Trust in the Lord with all your heart and lean not on your own understanding, in all your ways acknowledge him, and he will make your paths straight".* Chapter 3 v 5 & 6.

- *"My son, pay attention to what I say, listen closely to my words. Do not let them out of your sight; keep them within your heart, for they are life to those who find them and health to a man's whole body. Above all else, guard your heart, for it is the wellspring of life."* Chapter 4 v 20-23.

- *"For wisdom is more precious than rubies, and nothing you desire can compare with her"*. Chapter 8 v 11.

- *"A generous man will prosper, he who refreshes others will himself be refreshed "*. Chapter 11 v 25

- *"A cheerful look brings joy to the heart, and good news gives health to the bones"*. Chapter 15 v 30.

- *"Listen to advice and accept instruction, and in the end you will be wise"* Chapter 19 v 20.

- *"Do not wear yourself out to get rich, have the wisdom to show restraint. Cast but a glance at riches, and they are gone, for they will surely sprout wings and fly off to the sky like an eagle"* Chapter 23 v 4&5.

Here are ten things that may help you as you seek to put some direction in your life; particularly in midlife where you might find yourself 'stuck' meandering down to retirement.

1. Get alongside people you trust, who know where they are going, and have some direction for their lives.

2. Don't allow procrastination to rob you of making plans for your life. Take the first step today.

3. Stay away from cynical people, and the 'psychologically unplugged', rather listen to positive people, and those with vision.

4. Cultivate a habit of continually learning, reading helpful books, and taking in information.

5. Evaluate your life on a yearly basis, and determine progress on your objectives.

6. From time to time, don't be afraid to peruse areas of your life where you have achieved something. Get out your diplomas and certificates – this helps put things in perspective.

7. Learn from the word of God. You will find much direction for your life.

8. Be part of a great life filled Church where God is made famous, faith is part of every day life, the local community is influenced, and you are able to grow as a Christian.

9. Make a list of ten things you want to happen in the next year and write them down. Writing things down means you have something tangible to measure and it helps to fix things in your mind. It also enables you to see the areas you have changed and the areas that need more attention to enable change. This may involve a change of job. Be very specific about the type of job you would really like, the salary, and even the job description, and don't forget the fringe benefits. If it's a house move then again be specific about the type of house you would like to live in, including the surroundings. (Judy and I would like our next house to be near some water.) Don't forget to include some things about your family and their future health and happiness.

10. Finally, as said before, line up the lights for your life, and get all the help, wisdom, instruction and advice needed for this.

"There are risks and costs to a programme of action, but they are far less than the long-range risks and costs of comfortable inaction"

(John F. Kennedy, 1917 - 1963 President of the United States of America)

Chapter 4

Laugh and the World Laughs With You
(Eddie)

Laughter is a very serious matter. Being able to laugh at yourself, and with others, is a core ingredient to a healthy life. It has been said, *"A 100 chuckles a day keeps the doctor away"*. Researchers estimate that laughing 100 times a day is equal to a ten minute workout on a rowing machine. Research has also found that laughter reduces certain types of stress hormones which suppress the immune system. So laughter releases endorphins which give us the feel good factor, and, in turn, relaxes the whole body by reducing stress and tension. So if we believe *'laughter is the best medicine'* come on, we all ought to be doing more of it!

I was very interested recently in reading Daniel Goleman's book on emotional intelligence in leaders, pointing those of us in any form of leadership to relevant ways of connecting to people, and, in turn, motivating and inspiring them in their day-to-day work. I was interested, particularly, in the references to smiling, warmth and laughter, primarily because I have used these very important mediums, both in my working life as a team leader, in a social work setting, and in Church life as a pastoral leader.

Goleman, quoting a study at the Yale University School Of Management, found that "amongst working groups, cheerfulness and warmth spread most easily, whilst irritability is less contagious and depression spreads hardly at all". He goes on to say that laughter, in particular, demonstrates the power of the 'open loop' in operation, and, therefore, the contagious nature of all emotion. Hearing laughter, we automatically smile or laugh too, creating a spontaneous chain reaction that sweeps through a group. Glee spreads so readily because our brain includes open loop circuits, specifically for detecting smiles and laughter that make us laugh in response.

Robert Holden, in his book, 'Laughter the best medicine', says, "if negative thoughts, feelings and emotions can hold up health, what then can positive thoughts, feelings, and emotions achieve?". Could it be that an ability to laugh, the courage to smile, a propensity for hope and optimism, a readiness to radiate good humour and a playful disposition are healthful frames of mind that may accelerate healing and recovery from illness" So laughter, just like love, is an important key to the happiness, growth, and healing of us all.

It is true, that for many of us, we don't seem to have too much to laugh about, or we have forgotten how to laugh, smile and enjoy life. Perhaps we need to look at children, they instinctively learn how to smile, laugh and play. Hearing and visually impaired children smile. Children of all cultures smile. I am informed that a child smiles within the first six weeks of life, and, when discovered, will '*play with smiles all day long*'. If we encourage a child to smile, they will do it all the more. They learn that smiling will gain attention and help them to communicate, particularly with adults. Actually, I have found that 'grown-ups' can be encouraged to smile and enjoy. In working situations laughter can ease troubles and frustrations and help us focus on what is important.

We all had incidents in our lives that made us laugh or cry, particularly when we were children. In fact children can teach us much about fun, joy and laughter. Violet Oaklander, who has a Ph D in Clinical Psychology and who has won international recognition for her unique approach to working with children, writes in her book, "*Windows to our Children*: "*Children are our finest teachers. They already know how to grow, how to develop, how to learn, how to expand and discover, how to feel, laugh and cry and get mad, what is right for them, what they need. They already know how to love and be joyful and to live life to its fullest, to work and to be strong and full of energy. All they (and the children within us) need is the space to do it"*

An incident that Judy and I often reflect on, have a good laugh, can't really believe it happened, occurred about eighteen years ago when our eldest boy was 14 and our youngest was 8. We were on holiday on the banks of Loch Lomond in Scotland (which was actually the place where my ancestors – the Colquhoun family originated from). We were staying in a luxury pine cabin and, as always in Scotland, it was cold and wet. We decided to have a go at fishing on the loch, and hired a motor boat – that is actually a very grand description, for it was a basic rowing boat with an old outboard motor attached to it. We set off and explored the loch, put our lines in the water, and many hours later decided it could be time to return to our cabin, as there were no signs of any fish, and certainly not on our lines. On our journey back, in the distance, we noticed four 'red' flags (now that should have been a clue). The discussion went a bit like this-should we go around the flags or through them? My wife decided we should go through them so we headed towards the middle of the flags. As we went through the flags the boat went up on rocks. Like James Bond, I sprang up and lifted the out board motor clear of the rocks. At the same time the petrol poured completely over me. In the middle of the panic Richard, our eldest son, jumped on the rock and pushed the boat away from the rocks. As he jumped back in the boat he knocked the rollock into the water. Just as we were deciding what to do a cruiser style boat went by and the wash from the cruiser upturned our little boat. I changed from being James Bond into Captain Mannering from Dad's Army. I can remember saying to everyone "*don't panic, don't panic*". Judy wasn't panicking. She couldn't speak and she told me later that all her life flashed before her. She also remembered what the owner of the cabin had previously said, that the water was very deep and cold and had strong currents that would pull you under. When the boat stopped rocking I took a decision to start up the outboard motor. Well, the end of the story is that we did eventually arrive back at the cabin, me smelling of petrol and Judy already convinced that we would never go to Scotland on holiday again!

My very good friend and pastor, Chris Denham, said recently that "*destiny is determined by the choices you make*". I believe we can all make the choice today to laugh, smile and play, no matter how old we are. Let's begin and you will see something remarkable. Those around you - family, friends and colleagues, will respond more positively to you and to others.

Here is a poem by Leslie Gibson that encapsulates the importance of a smile.

A Smile

A smile costs nothing, but gives much. It enriches those who give it. It takes but a moment, but the memory of it sometimes lasts forever

None is so rich or mighty that he can get along without it, and none is so poor but that he cannot be made richer by it.

A smile creates happiness in the home, promotes goodwill in business, and is the cornerstone of friendship. It can perk up the weary, bring cheer to the discouraged, sunshine to the sad, and is nature's best remedy for trouble.

Yet it cannot be bought, begged, borrowed or stolen, for it is something that is of no value to anyone until it is given away.

When people are too tired to give you a smile, give them one of yours. No one needs a smile so much as he who has none to give.

(Leslie Gibson, RN BSN, is a speaker specializing in stress management and therapeutic humour techniques.)

I have found that smiling, and laughter in appropriate times and places, makes difficult situations bearable. Social workers sometimes feel the need to debrief together, discuss and laugh at situations and people they have encountered in their day-to- day work. They are not laughing at the people, but are giving permission for colleagues to be 'real' and let off the safety release valve.

Here is a true story that happened to us: a great illustration of a difficult situation which we have been able to laugh about since. One Saturday morning the aerial dropped off the roof, the kettle blew up and the iron stopped working and the washing machine started to pour water all over the kitchen floor. Could things get any worse? We were in the middle of trying to mop the water up from the floor when there was a knock at the door. It was our next door neighbour, very distressed, asking for help as his wife was behaving very strangely and he didn't know what to do. She was actually very ill and was having what we commonly call a nervous break-down. Did this put our small hiccups into perspective?

You bet it did. Although we didn't feel like smiling at the time we have often smiled about that day since.

There was another occasion that was not funny at the time but again we now often laugh about it.

My son and I were watching the World Cup with England playing. It went to extra time, still no score and it was now going to penalties. The atmosphere was tense and every one was holding their breath when suddenly there was a knock at the door. We all looked at the door. Should we ignore it and hope who ever it was would go away? Our son went to open the door. A very distressed lady, who looked extremely ill, literally fell through the door and said she was dying.

The look of horror on my son's face still makes me smile now. My son made his decision quickly and shot upstairs to his bedroom to finish watching the match. I hesitated for a minute and contemplated following him upstairs, but seeing my wife's expression decided to stay downstairs and offer support. I was also mouthing to my wife "who is it?"

This lady was part of a couple whom we had met previously on a few occasions. They lived abroad and have relatives that live close by to us. When they visited their relatives they would often call into see us. We had no idea that they were over in England, so her visit came completely out of the blue.

The good news is that after talking to her and giving her a drink we were able to get her some medical assistance. As a family we have often laughed about this situation and how it tested our pastoral heart.

Richard Briers in the television programme, 'Ever Decreasing Circles' said "*I have a smile growing inside me, but it will take a while to appear on my face*". A smile is far more attractive than a frown and it takes more muscles to frown than to smile so don't be like Richard Briers let the smile appear on your face don't keep it inside you.

Last year, as part of a Church outing, Judy and I went to see one of the students at our Church taking part in a modern day version of Shakespeare's 'Twelve Night' at Bretton Hall College as part of his final year degree production. It was a wonderful production. He did a great job. We were very proud of him. As it was a modern production the story was interpreted as, shall we say, a fruity love story. During the first half I was sitting next to our pastor's wife. She said she was very embarrassed during the love scenes as she felt like she was sitting next to her father. So she was really relieved that Judy sat next to her for the second half. Well, I think I laughed about that all night, and have done so many times since.

I love what Kate Hull Rogers in her book 'Pearls of Bizdom' said, commenting on humour and stress in the work place; *"Ill I think is an acronym for I lack laughter"*. Perhaps it is time for senior management of organisations within the UK to take note of the above comment. It is time to acknowledge that there is a tangible link between low staff morale, stress in the work place and high rates of staff absenteeism, both short and long term. We need to recognise that an ethos of humour, and good team spirit could indeed make noticeable inroads into affecting positively some of the above.

It is also true, and agreed by the authors of the One Minute Managers, that people who feel good about themselves produce good results

Dr Albert Ellis, founder of Rational Emotive Therapy, gives humour and fun its rightful place in psychotherapy. He noticed that people often disturb themselves with over-irrational, subjective and over -serious thinking. He describes this as: *'catastrophizing'*, *'awfulizing'*, *'terrible-izing'*, and *'horrible-izing'*. The ability to laugh at oneself in particular, is a vital psychological immunity against the modern thinking disease of 'over-seriousness'. He promotes laughter as a mental and emotional tool that can so often inspire a return to balanced, objective and rational thought.

Here are ten things to help you bring back fun, release, health and happiness to your life.

1. Don't take yourself so seriously. Lighten up a little, and remember, life is for living.

2. Practice laughter. Happiness is a muscle. It needs to be exercised and used regularly.

3. Understand that happiness is not something you are waiting for. It can be yours now. Simply step into it.

4. Laughter is something you need to share with others. So, go on, make a difference in your world and don't wait for others.

5. Keep learning. This will keep you young. There is always some thing new to learn, and to experience.

6. Understand that laughter, joy, and happiness are ways of living and should be part of your journey through life.

7. Learn to be thankful every day of your life. It will make you more forgiving, and less resentful of others.

8. Be a giver, there is nothing more refreshing and life-giving than a person who learns to give, even without receiving. (Proverbs 11v25).

9. Learn to feel good about yourself. It will actually make you produce better results and be more interesting in your relationships with others.

10. Finally, laugh and play.

"Laughter can relieve tension, soothe the pain of disappointment and strengthen the spirit for the formidable tasks that always lie ahead"

(Dwight D. Eisenhower 1890-1969 President of the United States of America.)

Chapter 5

Lost! Somewhere in Venice!

(Judy)

In 2007 I fulfilled my ambition to become a graduate. At the age of 53 I successfully completed an MA in Childhood Studies. July that year became the graduation celebration month. It started with a party when we celebrated with our friends the achievement of becoming an MA graduate. Then came the graduation day, It was a beautiful summer's day. The Leeds Metropolitan University looked at its best with the grounds in front of the main building laid out with tables and chairs, huge marquees and various stalls. Helpful stewards directed the visitors around the campus.

When we arrived we were taken to collect the tickets and robes. I was helped into the robe and mortar board. It was all a bit surreal. Was this really me? Then off for the official photograph. Outside in the grounds were other students with their proud families. At 1:30pm we were ushered into the huge marquee for the ceremony. Waiting at the side of the stage for my name to be called and then making my way across the platform to be presented to Brendan Foster, the Chancellor of the University, is a memory that I will never forget. That was it! The moment- when I officially graduated. This was what all the hard work had been for. Following the ceremony we passed from one marquee into another where there was a buffet and a band was playing. As it was such a lovely day families were going out onto the lawn with their food. I enjoyed watching the proud families celebrating together and enjoying that special day.

As a treat my husband had booked a weekend in Venice to celebrate. When we returned from the graduation ceremony we packed, ready to set off early the next morning to fly to Venice. Our flight left Leeds Bradford Airport at 6.00am on time and we arrived at Marco Polo airport at 11.00am their time. We arrived at the hotel, which was right on the Grand Canal by water taxi, checked in and wasted no time changing into our shorts and t shirts and set off to explore the delights of St Marks Square and the Rialto bridge. It was extremely hot and we were grateful to keep going into air conditioned shops or a shady alley way to get out of the sun for a while.

After a great afternoon we decided to head back to the hotel. After half an hour we were sure that we had just walked round in a circle and were getting nowhere fast. We set off in another direction but every where looked the same; bridges over water, little alleyways, canals, and shops with Venetian glass, ornate Venetian masks and little cafés. We had drunk three bottles of water, my feet felt like raw meat and my face was beginning to glow. My map did not have street names on so I had no idea where we were. Help! Lost somewhere in Venice!

People can feel lost in many different situations particular in mid life. They feel 'lost' in their career, and unable to keep up with all the constant changes that occur in this modern age of technology. They are unable to cope with computer programmes, emails, web sites, blackberries and texting and changes in *'management styles'*, which these days seem to include *'hot desking'*, multi-tasking, and the sacrifice of individualism in organisations.

In relationships, there can be a sense of being lost in the routines of married life, and sameness, highlighted in a cautious attitude towards taking risks or meeting new challenges such as further education, or travelling to far flung places that would broaden minds. Sometimes between the ages of 50 and 55, with the advent of the pensionable age looming in the not too distant future, there is a danger of becoming old in attitude, opinion, and, most worryingly, in losing that lightness of spirit that helps to keep us young at heart.

It is easy in a Church situation to become *'lost'* in your mission and service and to become caught up in Church politics which do nothing to help build the kingdom of God or reach out to the lost. We need to regularly assess what we are doing in Church. It is so easy to become a religious social club when our mission is to reach those who are needy, hurting or lost.

Do you sometimes feel lost, not sure where you're heading, feel like you are going round in circles? Then here are ten things to help in these situations.

1. Ask someone who has a good knowledge of God and a track record to prove it to help you find direction for your life. We eventually found our way back to the hotel because we asked some one to help us to point us in the right direction.

2. Start to do something different! Don't carry on being lost. We could have carried on wandering round Venice but we made a decision to do something about being lost.

3. God has called each of us for a purpose; seek Him about what your purpose is.

4. Make plans to change. Enrol on a course! Start language lessons!

5. Don't procrastinate. You can stop being lost today!

6. Use the greatest map book for your life the Bible. The Bible tells us to *"Trust in the Lord with all your heart and he will direct our paths."* (Proverbs 3 v 5)

7. Start to be specific. If you are making changes and praying about them, be specific with God. It also focuses your mind about what you are looking to change.

8. Plan to do something special and pleasurable on a regular basis!

9. Believe in your ability to take on new challenges. God has promised that he has given us everything we need to live a life of godliness.

10. Recognise that being lost will rob you of your joy and confidence.

*"Those with a lively sense of
curiosity learn something new
every day of their lives."*
(Anonymous)

Chapter 6

You Could Be a Priceless Antique

(Eddie and Judy)

Just because you may be a little chipped around the edges it does not mean that you have no worth. Experience and wisdom can not be gained from a book or a university course. Experience comes from trying things, making mistakes, learning from them and having successes.

Alan Sugar, in his book "How to be an Apprentice", states that many organisations and companies have, as their figure head, a man or woman of 60+ years. He explains why that is by saying, "*they've listened to every salesman, every marketing person, every engineer, and every production planner. They've absorbed the valleys and mountains of industrial disaster, financial collapse, economic downturn and political change. They've seen it all, so they know what to do. You can't replace that. You can't get that degree of experience and knowledge out of a can, and you can't buy it in a book. You can't put old heads on young shoulders*".

Recently the retail industry has also recognised that employing older, even semi- retired people, can be of enormous benefit. B&Q have deliberately recruited people over 50 as they are able to give customers advice about how to use different tools, give demonstrations about how to 'do it yourself' and can advise customers of the best product for the job they are tackling.

The generation gap is not a part of God's ideal world! The true Church is intergenerational, where young, middle and older members respect and value the unique contribution that they all bring. In our Church we have a number of students and, for many, this is their first time away from home. One of the things that the older members can do is cook for the students. The students love nothing better than eating home cooked food. Some times they need mothers and fathers in the house who will love and believe in them and encourage them to seek God's best for their life. Could you just give a hug, a word of encouragement, a text or phone call to a lonely young person? There are so many jewels that you could give out to young people.

The Bible has lots to say about wisdom:
"Blessed is the man who finds wisdom, the man who gains understanding, for she is more profitable than silver and yields better returns than gold."

Proverbs Chapter 3 v 13

"Wise men store up knowledge, but the mouth of the fool invites ruin."

Proverbs Chapter 10 v 14

"Listen to advice and accept instruction and in the end you will be wise."

Proverbs Chapter 19 v 20

"Listen to your father, who gave you life, and do not despise your mother when she is old. Buy the truth and do not sell it; get wisdom, discipline and understanding."

Proverbs Chapter 23 v 22

"Those who are wise will shine like the brightness of the heavens, and those who lead many to righteousness like the stars for ever and ever."

Daniel Chapter 12 v 3

Why don't you choose to be a hero in the faith to the young people that you come across? Young people need us to believe in them. They need us to pick them up when they stumble and fall and get them back on track.

It does not matter how old you are! If you are still breathing you can be an encourager and a refresher to others!

Here are ten pearls of wisdom you can give to others!

1. No one is perfect. Everyone makes mistakes. The person, that never made a mistake never made anything. The positive thing to do is to learn from your mistakes and don't make them again.

2. People will disappoint you but you need to learn to deal with disappointment and carry on.

3. Don't give up. If you don't achieve your goal the first time, try again.

4. An encouraging word can make all the difference. Hebrews Chapter 3 v 13 says: "*But encourage one another daily, as long as it is called today, so that none of you may be hardened by sin's deceitfulness*".

5. Work hard and play hard and you will be rewarded in health and wealth.

6. The world encourages you to rely on your own understanding and where you think you need to go. Where as in God's kingdom the Bible tells in Proverbs Chapter 3 vs 5: "*Trust in the Lord with all your heart*

and lean not on your own understanding and He will direct your paths."

7. Everyone needs a friend. Be loyal, supportive and caring in the good times and the bad.

8. A problem shared is a problem halved. Find someone you can trust and let them share the load. Sometimes when you are in the middle of a crisis you can't see a way out, but someone else, however, can help and support you along the way!

9. Relationships are really important. When God created Adam he knew there was something missing. Adam needed someone he could have a relationship with and he created Eve. From the beginning of time God desired to have a relationship with man. Relationships can bring us joy and pain, but we can not survive without them.

10. If you don't want to experience hurt and pain then don't love. If you want a close relationship with someone, where you open your heart. Then expect both blissful joy and a little disappointment! The two very often go together.

Chapter 7

Don't Be a Wrinkled Dried-Up Prune!
Be a Juicy Grape!

(Judy)

I suspect that being refreshing has nothing at all to do with age, environment, background, money, status or life experience, or academic qualifications, but indeed more about the spirit of a person, and the culture that they live in and pursue.

Proverbs chapter 11 v 25 is a favourite verse in the Bible and says, *"A generous man will prosper; he who refreshes others will himself be refreshed."*

I guess I couldn't talk about refreshing without mentioning the Zimmers! In case you didn't know, they are quoted as being *"a rock band of 40 old aged pensioners with more aggression than Nirvana and more style than the Who!"* A few years back the Zimmers worked with a top music producer at the famous Abbey Road Studio and recorded an extraordinary version of the Who's *"My Generation"*. They also did a TV show about them. One of the things the program about them did was to challenge the preconceptions we all have about the elderly. These 'older people' are indeed 'young at heart', and took us all on a rock and roll journey.

It is always fantastic to see an older person, living outside the box and refusing to be pigeonholed and restricted in what they should do or think. The following stories wonderfully illustrate that age does not necessarily have to dictate how creative we can be in our thinking and our actions

Alec

I once read the story of Alec Holden who had recently turned 100. Alec has two sons, aged 70 and 60. Ten years ago he placed a wager with William Hill bookmakers that he would live to be a hundred! The bet was £100, and the odds were 100 to 1. You've guessed right, today Alec picked up £25,000. Alec plans to have a holiday in Eastbourne, and be 'waited on hand and foot'. When asked about his secrets for living to 100, Alec replied, "I do as little work as possible, get as many holidays as I can and have porridge for breakfast and, of course, you need to keep breathing- that's essential." How wonderful is the human spirit when it is not shackled by convention, age or environment!

Alice

Alice is 92 and has experienced a more difficult and troublesome life than most of us. She has had issues with poor housing, financial and personal difficulties and had many years of caring for elderly relatives.

For many years Alice lived on a caravan site frequented by gypsies and travellers. One of her normal routines was to go shopping to the local supermarket with her 90 year old friend, who happened to be a gypsy. On their return from the supermarket, Alice would ring the bus bell to ask the driver to stop at the appropriate place near their home. The driver would ignore Alice's request to stop the bus at their stop, and drive perhaps another 200metres further up the road, leaving Alice and her friend a long walk back laden down with bags of shopping.

This had gone on for some time. Alice had enough of this prejudiced behaviour and decided to stand up to the bus driver. The next time Alice and her friend were returning from the supermarket she rang the bell and asked the driver to stop the bus. The bus driver remarked "I can't hear you. Speak up". Without losing her dignity Alice said, "I have your name and your number and I will be informing the bus company that they have a driver who is deaf and unable to do his job". Suffice to say she had no more trouble from this driver. The driver, from then on, always stopped the bus at their stop. Determination will get you where you need to go! Even at 92 years young!

Someone once said *"Youth is not an age, it is an attitude"* this is very true! So how do we keep our spirits fresh? How do we stop ourselves becoming stale and irrelevant? We have to be prepared to allow ourselves to be constantly changed and renewed.

The Bible tells us why this is important:

"No-one tears a patch from a new garment and sews it on an old one. If he does, he will have torn the new garment, and the patch from the new will not match the old. And no-one pours new wine into old wineskins. If he does, the new wine will burst the skins, the wine will run out and the wineskins will be ruined. No, new wine must be poured into new wineskins."

(NIV Bible Luke chapter 5 v 36-38).

The trouble with anything new is as soon as you use it the item is no longer new. I have a shoe fetish and love purchasing new shoes. How great they look, all shiny and sparkly in the box with no scuffs or scratches, but as soon as you wear them they are not new any more. The perfectly shiny, smooth soles develop scratches and are dirty from pounding the pavements.

So how do you keep your wine skin new? Is it enough to try and keep up with the latest fashion or to sing the latest worship songs in Church? That's a start, but that can become as much of a liturgy as singing hymns. It is so easy for us to fall into routines and rituals. We need to keep in mind what our purpose and mission is. The world needs us to be relevant to them now; so we have to be prepared to continually develop and change to keep our wine skins new, flexible and able to contain the new wine that God has for us.

God cannot pour in the fullness of His Spirit if we are living on yesterday's blessing. God is looking for new, flexible wineskins that are able to hold the new rivers of His blessing.
Here are ten ways to keep your wineskins new!

1. Keep a short account with God - have a daily relationship with Him.

2. Be prepared to change and carry on changing.

3. Be accountable to others.

4. Be excited about the future. Don't cling to the past.

5. Be willing to let go of position, routines and roles.

6. Be full of faith, expectation and hope for what God can do!

7. Set new goals, and dream new dreams.

8. Develop your character, God needs character and gifting to achieve his will.

9. Persevere to the end and receive a crown of righteousness!

10. Keep on being filled, renewed and refreshed.

"I am only one. But still I am one. I cannot do everything, but still I can do something. I will not refuse to do the something I can do"

(Helen Keller, 1880-1968 American Writer and Lecturer)

Chapter 8

Be a Risk Taker

(Eddie)

If we follow the natural course of events and ways of living we have learned from our parents and colleagues, many of us will end up living a safe, cautious, non- exciting, and 'boring' life, particularly as we approach that wonderful time called mid-life. The Daily Express ran an article looking at the differences between life in the 1950's and life in the new Millennium. Here are some startling factoids!

Subject	1957	2007
Length of retirement male	7.6 years	15 years
Length of retirement females	13. 9 years	22 years
Weekly spend	£199 per week *	£455 per week
Number of holidays/short breaks	1 to two a year	8 – 9 per year
Spend on holidays	£128 per year *	£845 per year
Main daily activities (excluding media consumption)	Cleaning and tidying	Shopping and socialising
Divorce rate	1 in 450 couples	1 in 58 couples

* Taking account of inflation

Psychologist Martin Lloyd-Elliot once said: "Today, 50 is closer to the middle of our life than its end". Psychologically, there has been a shift from a 'closing down' expectation for the second half of life, towards a more optimistic 'opening of doors' spirit of good times ahead. He goes on to say: "in fact, the life of a 50-something in 2007 is thought to be so packed with fun and so far removed from that of their counterparts of 50 years ago that researchers of the Future Foundation believe they'd give 1957's 20-somethings a run for their money."

Perhaps it is time for us all to have a rethink about our life styles, and how they are fashioned, and who is it, that dictates to us how we should live! It seems to me that economic circumstances have dramatically changed for the 50-somethings. Generally we enjoy better health, we are able to access higher education and travel to places our parents couldn't have dreamed of.

Someone once wisely said: "Our lives are not determined by what happens to us but by how we react to what happens, not by what life brings us, but by the attitude we bring to life. A positive attitude causes a chain reaction of positive thoughts, events, and outcomes. It is a catalyst and, a spark that creates extraordinary results".

On one particular night, whilst leading a small home group, we found ourselves talking about risk - taking, persevering and not giving up. One of the young women in the group had just received her A' level results and they were much lower than she expected. In fact her place at university was now in question. Struggling with feelings of failure, she had to make a decision whether to take the exams again or settle for the lower grades. She was very distressed and couldn't see the way ahead. It came to me instinctively that all of the people in the room had failed in some way. I encouraged the young woman with this, and urged her, to take the A' levels again, with a new sense of expectation. Well the end of the story is that the young woman did take the exams again and this time attained good results. Where is she now? Well she is the deputy head in one of the most prestigious schools in the North of England.

Perhaps one of the greatest examples of persistence in history was that of Abraham Lincoln. He was faced with defeat throughout his life; he lost eight elections, twice failed in business and suffered a nervous breakdown. However he never gave up.

Here is a list of Abraham Lincoln's journey to the White House!

1816   His family was forced out of their home. He had to work to support them.

1818   His mother died.

1831   He failed in business.

1832   Ran for legislature and lost.

1832   Lost his job; wanted to go to law school but couldn't get in.

1833   Borrowed some money from a friend to begin a business and by the end of the year he was bankrupt. He spent the next 17 years of his life paying off this debt.

1834   Ran for legislature again; this time won.

1835   Was engaged to be married, sweetheart died and his heart was broken.

1836   Had a total nervous breakdown and was in bed for six months.

1838   Sought to become speaker of the state legislature and was defeated.

1840   Sought to become elector and was defeated.

1843   Ran for Congress and lost.

1846   Ran for Congress again, and this time he won. He went to Washington and did a good job.

1848   Ran for re-election to Congress and lost.

1849   Sought the job of land officer in his home state and was rejected.

1854   Ran for Senate of the United State and lost.

1856   Sought the Vice-Presidential nomination at his party's national convention; he got less than 100 votes.

1858   Ran for U.S. Senate again and, again, he lost.

1860   Was elected a President of the United States.

Abraham Lincoln once stated after losing a race for the senate: "The path was worn and slippery. My foot slipped from under me, knocking the other out of the way, but I recovered and said to myself: 'it is a slip and not a fall.'

Sometimes you have to be prepared to take a risk even when people with some kind of authority are telling you it is not worth it. Rob Law was a contestant in the television programme 'Dragons Den'. He had designed a brightly coloured children's suitcase, which doubled as a ride on wheelie toy. The Dragons Den Panellists were merciless in their criticism, with one panel member declaring the product to be completely worthless. One year on and 85,000 sales later, Rob's company is booming and selling to 22 countries. The 'Trunki' is an unequivocal hit, recently named as one of the best selling products in John Lewis department stores. The value of his company grew quickly to be in excess of £1million pounds. Where would he have been if he had left the Dragons Den and given up on his original idea? Sometimes you have to be prepared to take a risk and swim against the odds to succeed.

A close friend of ours, Paul Owen, made a major change of career in his middle forties. He had, for some time worked, in the coal mine, but, during the miners strike in 1984 decided to take a risk and go back to University. He studied for a Bachelor of Science degree in Fishery Studies, and specialised in Food Science after one year. On leaving University he was successful straight away in obtaining a position with a mushroom grower and then was head hunted by a National Salad grower. This job took him all over the world and eventually gave him the opportunity, at 60, to relocate to Gran Canaria. He has recently, at the age of 65, won a prize for the "Best Importer Of The Year" for the new joint venture company called Spania Fresh Canarias. It imports tomatoes, cucumbers and peppers for the UK's supermarkets. If that wasn't enough, listen to what his wife Kay achieved! At the age of 38 she had twins, re-trained as a chiropodist and went on to become the head chiropodist of a local authority! At the age of 54 she ran a very successful private chiropody practice. In Gran Canaria, they both took on positions of responsibility within the evangelical Church, and both of them have embraced the Canarian life and learned to speak fluently in Spanish. Not bad for two mid-lifers.

So who knows what is in store for you!

Here are ten things to remember when taking a risk:

1. We need to pay attention to the future. That's where we will spend the rest of our lives, and remember, the future starts with you today.

2. Let life become an adventure, not a series of problems.

3. Understand that we all have an overwhelming potential to be better.

4. Step out of your 'comfort zones', and do something different such as going on a mission, further education, being generous or reaching out to your local community.

5. Set yourself some big goals or you'll always do what you've always done, and get what you've always got. You are worth more!

6. Have a positive expectation of achieving your goals and the resilience to 'keep going'.

7. Be careful about the language you use. Keep it purposeful and affirming, not cynical and destructive.

8. Don't accept 'good enough'. But raise your own standards, and accept responsibility for your expectations.

9. Accept the challenge, and enlarge your capacity to see things different. Stretch yourself.

10. Look for the natural creativity that God has given you, don't let what you can't do interfere with what you can do.

"A lot of successful people are risk-takers. Unless you're willing to do that- to have a go, fail miserably, and have another go, success won't happen".

(Philip Adams, b. 1939 Australian Writer and Radio Broadcaster)

Chapter 9

Use Your Tongue to Build, Not Destroy
(Judy)

You may have seen a series of programmes on the TV called 'Grumpy Old Men' or 'Grumpy Old Women' where celebrities have a good old moan about the things they don't like. The Victor Meldrew spirit has become a stereo type for older people and it is very easy to slip into this kind of mindset. Nothing today is as good as it was when they were young. Relationships were better, food was better, music was better etc.

When people are reminiscing I find they are often wearing their rose- tinted glasses about the past. They very rarely remember the awful things that happened. People in my family fondly recall Church outings to Scarborough in the 50's. The films taken at the time, however, show us sitting on the beach wearing winter jumpers, coats, hats and scarves! We were freezing cold, sitting, eating potted meat sandwiches filled with sand, and blown about by the wind! Living in the past is not helpful if you want to be relevant to people today! I personally think there is nothing more unattractive than a grumpy person who has nothing positive to say, but is full of moans and groans!

We all can choose our attitude! We can choose to use our tongues to build or to destroy. Proverbs, Chapter 12 v 19 says "*reckless words pierce like a sword but the tongue of the wise brings healing*". There is a saying: '*sticks and stones may break my bones but words will never hurt me'*. How wrong that is! Words can be extremely hurtful and can have a lasting affect if we let them.

A few years back Gerard Keehan (the original Pioneer of Hillsong Church, London) once said that it takes one hundred positive words to undo one negative word. If that is true, we all have to try harder to not say that one negative word! One of my teachers wrote in my school report, "If her pen was as fluent as her tongue she would do well!" I have never forgotten those words. Thankfully, I can now laugh about it but it is amazing how words can pierce our spirit. How many of us, when we are having a disagreement, lose our cool and say reckless things that we would not normally say? If we want to be wise then we should use our tongue to bring healing.

James, Chapter 3v3–6 describes how powerful the tongue is: "*When we put bits into the mouths of horses to make them obey us, we can turn the whole animal. Or take ships as an example. Although they are so large and are driven by strong winds, they are steered by a very small rudder, wherever the pilot wants to go. Likewise the tongue is a small part of the body, but it makes great boasts. Consider what a great forest is set on fire by a small spark. The tongue also is a fire, a world of evil among the parts of the body. It corrupts the whole person, sets the whole course of his life of his life on fire, and is itself set on fire by hell". (Message)*

How we use our tongue, and the words we use over our world, is also important. If we speak negative things over our lives then we can expect negative things to happen. Negativity, cynicism and unbelief kill faith, and the Bible tells us that without faith it is impossible to please God.

It is really easy when we get older to develop a judgemental spirit. Just because we are older does not mean to say that we are always wiser or have the right approach. We can judge people by the way they dress and behave! I can remember in the 70's wearing tiny mini skirts and Eddie wearing two toned loons that the older people at the time spoke out strongly against. Judgemental attitudes can destroy dreams, drive wedges between generations, and can kill excitement and expectation about the future.

Here are ten ways to use your tongue to build a positive future:

1. Be an encourager. You can always find something positive to say to people. Start to change negative statements into positive ones.

2. Choose to speak positively over your life.

3. Refuse to be judgemental towards others. Always highlight people's strengths. Get them motivated and believe for the best in people.

4. Refuse to be grumpy old men/women. It is not attractive to the young at heart.

5. Talk up situations rather than making them small.

6. Avoid cynicism. It is subtle, but destructive.

7. Don't use banter (saying things supposedly in fun) that you actually mean.

8. Speak words of life into people.

9. If you haven't got anything positive to say then don't say anything!

10. Be a good listener, then you will respond more appropriately.

"Optimists are the elixir of life. They constantly remind the pessimists that life isn't as hopeless as they think. They are the extra ingredient that makes life bubble."

(Sara Henderson, b. 1936. Australian Outback Station

Manager and Writer)

Chapter 10

Can We Achieve a Good Work- Life Balance in Mid-Life?

(Eddie)

We hear much these days about a 'good work life balance', flexible working, changes in technology, productivity and absenteeism, and the notion of 'work related stress'. We are told now that stress has overtaken the common cold as the number one reason for workplace absenteeism. How different the world of work is now to my Dad's time when he walked to the local colliery with his flask of tea and sandwiches to sustain him during his hard toil underground. Coming home at the end of the day and not giving work another thought.

Obviously the technology was very limited, compared to today's innovations, but because the market was more labour intensive, and working at home was unheard of, home was where you went to have a rest at the end of the working day.

We are told that 'younger' workers coming into the labour market have very different attitudes towards the work ethics of the previous generation, and the 'generation X' (born between 1965 and 1980) are more likely to challenge the ethos of 'working long hours' than their parents ever did.

They are, conversely, more likely to stay in their jobs if the employer makes provision for a 'good work life balance'. According to 'The Work Foundation', work-life balance is achieved when an individual's right to a fulfilled life inside and outside paid work is accepted and respected as the norm, to the mutual benefit of the individual, business and society.

They go on to say that a 'good work-life balance' business benefits include:

- Increased productivity.
- Improved recruitment and retention.
- Lower rates of absenteeism.
- Reduced overheads.
- An improved customer experience.
- A more motivated, satisfied and equitable workforce.

We have an increasingly ageing population, with potentially, 12 million over 65's by 2021. This means that there will be 2.7 workers to every 1 non-worker (compared to 4:1 in 1990). We will have 3 million more workers over the age of 35. Up to 10 million people will be caring for elderly relatives (mainly women). Therefore as we see the demographic trends changing there will be more need for a realistic look, both as employers and employees, at a 'good work life balance' in the very near future.

Here are ten useful ways to maintain a good work life balance in your mid life, and to keep 'young at heart':

1. When you are at work do a good day's work for your employer. It can be equally stressful, not being organised or productive! And when you are at home play hard and have lots of fun.

2. On the way home from work focus on a good thing that happened at work. We can naturally, and only too easily, only focus on the negative aspects.

3. Have a lunch every day of at least half an hour away from your desk and work place. (I have given this advice over many years in training and I know from feedback that it is useful and helpful in addressing stress.)

4. Cultivate a number of hobbies and pastimes that we can enjoy away from work, i.e. walking (good for your

health), trips to the theatre or cinema (helps keep you relevant, as well as reading.) We have already encouraged you to read at least ten books a year! It will keep your mind alive. The list can be endless and, if you are a couple, do some of them together!

5. If you are in your 50's have regular well- woman or well- men check- ups. It makes really good sense to check your blood pressure, cholesterol levels, weight etc.

6. Try and eat out at a restaurant at least once a month and have some weekends away at a nice hotel every so often. Your wife/husband will love you for it.

7. Give support, and praise to your peers and to those in management, and learn to accept it in return. Don't be suspicious and cynical at work. People actually do, generally, mean what they say!

8. Recognise that you are middle-aged. Although you are young at heart, your body is not! So be sensible. Drink alcohol moderately, eat healthily, and take gentle exercise every day.

9. Be well organised in your life and use good time management skills to order your day (i.e. get up 15minutes earlier than usual to deal with things that are important first). Never lose spontaneity -; it keeps things fresh and alive.

10. Finally, laugh and play and try to see the funny side of things. It will make you live longer.

"If you can walk, you can dance, if you can talk, you can sing". (Zimbabwean Proverb)

"I think the biggest disease the world suffers from in this day and age is the disease of people feeling unloved. I know that I can give love for a minute, for half and hour, for a day, for a month, but I can give. I am happy to do that, I want to do that." (Princess Diana)

Chapter 11

What We Do While Living,

Echoes in Eternity!

(Eddie)

It is true that what we do in this life will 'echo in eternity'. As for Judy and me, we are grateful to God for the abundant life he has given us, as well as the promise of eternal life. It's not because of our good works, but because of our faith in Jesus

Christ. We believe, also that there is a crown of righteousness for those who fight the good fight and finish the race that God has marked out for us all.

I am convinced that we don't live in a vacuum. What we do, whether it is in action or attitude, certainly affects others and, most of all, ourselves. I heard many years ago that a certain manager in an organisation had such a negative and debilitative effect on colleagues that they instinctively knew what 'mood' the manager was in even by the manner in which she drove into the car park! We are all influenced by something all of the time, whether it be, negative talk, cynicism, suspicion or, conversely, words of encouragement, affirmations, or a culture of thankfulness and faith.

I believe that it is so important to recognise the culture we find ourselves in, particularly in our mid-life. I would like to draw out some 'ways of being' that will affect how we live and how we relate to the people around us.

I have noticed on many occasions that some older people seem to have lost their joy, laughter, freshness of spirit, and thankfulness for what they have in life. In so many cases, we see people who have become bitter, estranged, and feeling that the life that has been dealt to them is not a good one.

I want to suggest that we can determine much of how we live later on in life by the way we live now, in mid- life. Our older years will be affected by the attitudes that currently motivate and guide us.

Like any other area of life in our mid- life, there is a need to 'prepare' physically, emotionally, and spiritually for the next part of our life. It will be very different from the previous one in that our working life may decrease or come to an end, hobbies and pastimes may increase, and more time will be spent with our spouses, and wider family.

As mid-lifers we need to prepare how and where we should live. We may feel the need to move into a home that will better supply our needs in terms of mobility. This will require a degree of honesty. We advise parents to communicate with their children on this matter and listen to their views, as they will have some involvement in later years. It is important also to live in an area where there is a social network of friends, clubs or Church. This will take a degree of planning and will involve finances so help from various sources will be needed. These days it seems to be very common for mid-lifers to 'downsize', either to release cash for their retirement, or, in some cases, to help children buy their first house.

Emotionally, it is helpful to move into the next part of our lives being thankful, generous of spirit, and gracious. It is such a joy to see an older person who is truly thankful for their life and still want to contribute, both in opinion and in the way they give of themselves to others. There have been a number of older people in this category that have positively influenced me by the way that they have thought of others before themselves. They have left a great example for those around them of what it is to be generous of spirit!

In a spiritual sense it is good as mid-lifers that we don't put our feet up but continue to be an example to the young. So many young people nowadays need mothers and fathers in the faith. They need us to look up to.

So here are ten ways we can positively prepare for the next part of our lives.

1. Give some real thought and preparation to the next part of your life.

2. Openly and honestly discuss with your children your plans for the future.

3. Read literature that is helpful on the subject.

4. Think about downsizing or moving to a bungalow, if needed.

5. Don't stop being a giver of yourselves, and, stay fresh.

6. Get alongside people who are positive and will encourage you.

7. Get some good advice, regarding your finances and your future.

8. Continue to make a useful contribution, whether it is voluntary work, in your family, or in your Church life.

9. Give thanks every day of your life as this will keep you sweet.

10. Don't forget, also, to laugh and to play.

"Learning should be a joy and full of excitement, it is life's greatest adventure, it is an illustrated excursion into the minds of noble and learned men, not a conducted tour through a jail."

Taylor Caldwell, 1900-1985 American Writer.

Chapter 12

Please Can You Airbrush

the Bad Bits Out?

(Eddie)

Wouldn't it be great if we could 'airbrush' out parts of our life that we are not particularly happy with! These days celebrities, through air brushing photography, can have their blemishes removed, teeth whitened, and their bodies made to look thinner to present a perfect image to the world. So when your hair starts to turn a different colour or drop out, and when your face develops deep wrinkles, wouldn't it be great to look in the mirror and see an air brushed version?

We have news for you! When you look in the mirror, don't look away! That is the way you are meant to look at the age you currently are! Sorry to be a killjoy but real joy comes by facing real reality, not turning away from it.

So what is this new obsession with 'airbrushing' out the bad bits we don't like? We have found this phenomenon particularly with older people when talking about their past. It all sounds so rosy, wonderful and family orientated. The real picture is, in some cases, less rosy, and much more grounded in reality. It seems to me that the last generation kept more secrets than this generation, in order to cope with their lives. 'Airbrushing' is not a new phenomenon!

This funny little story is something that happened to me when I was eight or nine years old and it well illustrates how, from time to time, we have the need to cover the bad bits rather than facing reality.

It was Friday morning in my little village in Dumfriesshire. At the end of the week there was no money left. Dad's wages were needed to provide food for the family. A week's wages was a five pound note. My mum sent me with the crisp new five pound note to the local cooperative store for bread rolls and jam for breakfast. I hurriedly set off on this task as I had school to attend following breakfast. On my route to the store, the unbelievable happened - I lost the five pound note! For the next twenty minutes or so that seemed like a lifetime, I searched and searched for that crisp new five pound note, but I couldn't find it. The reality of the situation hit me I knew that I would have to face my mum. I had lost a whole week's wage and I knew I would be in big trouble.

I slowly returned home to receive what was coming to me. As I told my sad tale to my mum the look on her face communicated very adequately what was going to happen to me and I am sure she reached for something to hit me with. Before anything could happen I ran off in the direction of the Cooperative store. Then the next unbelievable thing happened! My eye was caught by a flickering piece of paper. It was the crisp new five pound note which had lodged itself on the side of a wooden garage not too far from my house.

Imagine how I felt! One minute I thought my family would have nothing to eat all week. The next minute I had found the lost five pound note! I can laugh about it now but, at the time, I would have rather this situation had not happened. Sometimes, when we face up to reality, we find that the things we fear are not as bad as we thought they would be.

One of the areas I have been very involved in my role as counsellor in an Education Department is that of giving support, advice and counsel to the bereaved. This has involved taking a team of workers into a school situation to offer guidance, support and counsel to pupils, school staff, and parents where there has been a death, or multiple deaths, in a school. There is a lot of skill involved in working in this field but perhaps the greatest, and most needed skill, is to be honest and just to 'be there for the person'. People who have been bereaved often say to me that they want other people to be honest with them, not to skirt round the subject or pass by on the other side of the road. It is facing up the realities of life, even in situations we wouldn't choose to find our selves in, which enables us to carry on and often become stronger people.

Some years ago I was privileged to spend a placement as a student social worker in Wakefield Hospice. This experience changed my approach towards counselling. Here I found real people who were called upon to face difficult times in their life with dignity, having to cope with the 'bad bits' that they wouldn't necessarily choose. I guess it was there that I began to learn that counselling was more than a set of skills or a process of just using all of the theories I'd been taught. It was more about me as a genuine real person, interacting with real people at the point of their need.

Facing up to these difficult circumstances, and being involved with others in crisis situations, had a great impact on my life and practice as a social worker.

Stop trying to hide the real you and be proud of who you are, bad bits and all – they make you unique. So here are ten ways you can say goodbye to the airbrush:

1. Don't try and be someone else. It will never work. Just be yourself!

2. Try and have at least one conversation a day where you can be really honest.

3. Present the same 'picture' of yourself whether you are at work, at home or at leisure.

4. Remember that you are fearfully and wonderfully made! You're of great worth to God! (NIV Bible Psalm 139 v 14)

5. Read books and autobiographies about real people. I recommend Jane and Mike Tomlinson's book "The Luxury of Time". It will really inspire you as you read about two ordinary people who faced a great challenge with extraordinary courage.

6. Take the time just to reflect on how your life is going!

7. Open up our life to others around you. Why not invite your neighbours round for coffee and a chat!

8. When you send Christmas cards don't just put love and your names. Try to write something about yourself or about what you have done recently. It will make a big difference!

9. When you are in conversation, use the term 'I', so you will own what you are saying.

10. Finally, don't be too hard on yourself. Be gentle with yourself. Treat yourself as well as you have ever treated the one you've loved the most. Treat yourself with compassion, high expectations, forgiveness and delight.

*"Whether living alone is adventure or hardship
will depend entirely on your attitude and your
decisions. Become friends with yourself; learn
to appreciate who you are and your unique gifts.
Be patient with yourself and use your sense of
humour to keep things in perspective."*

(Dorothy Edgerton, b. 1911 American Writer.)

Chapter 13

The Best Is Yet To Come

(Judy)

Since we have become part of the family of Hope City Church, our lives have been turned, but not upside down, the right way up. So many areas of our lives seem to make sense now. Lightness has come into our spirit and physically, mentally and spiritually, we have come to life! There has been a theme, and almost a catchphrase, for our lives that motivates us, encourages us, and directs us to all that God has for us. That catchphrase is 'the best is yet to come!'

As I think about this catchphrase I am convinced that it should be a catchphrase for so many mid-lifers, who are realising for the first time that their lives have just begun! There is within all of us the ability to be creative, to reach out and dream for greater things, not to be limited by convention, or tradition and to be all that God intended us to be! There is a challenge for us, as mid-lifers to break free of being 'pigeonholed' into the 'straightjacket' of mediocrity and sameness and to stretch ourselves and believe that there is so much more for each of us!

Recently I read a brilliant poem by Edgar Albert Guest (1881-1959), which in many ways emphasises what we have been trying to say all the way throughout this book. He explains that within all of us there is the possibility of being 'great' if only we change the way we think.

Somebody said that it couldn't be done, but he with
a chuckle replied,
That maybe it couldn't,
But he would be one
Who wouldn't say so till he tried.

So he buckled right in
With the trace
Of a grin on his face
If he worried,
He hid it.
He started to sing
As he tackled the thing,
That couldn't be done,
And he did it!

Somebody scoffed:
"Oh you'll never do that;
At least no one has ever done it".
But he took off his coat

And he took off his hat,
And the first thing we knew,
He'd begun it.

With a lift of his chin,
And a bit of a grin,
Without any doubting or quid it.
He started to sing
As he tackled the thing,
That couldn't be done,
And he did it!

There are thousands to tell you
It cannot be done.
There are thousands to prophesy failure!
There are thousands to point out to you,
One by one, the dangers that wait to assail you.
But just buckle in with a bit of a grin;
Just take off your coat and go to it.
Just start to sing,
As you tackle the thing,
That cannot be done
And you'll do it!"

We sincerely hope, and pray, that reading this little book will have inspired you to look deeper into yourself, to remember your Creator and to reach out to become all that you were intended to be. So why don't you come on this journey with us? Why settle for less than the best? Who knows what amazing destiny God has in store for you!

Finally, here are ten ways to ensure and believe that that the best is yet to come in you life.

1. *"Trust in the Lord with all your heart and lean not on your own understanding. In all your ways acknowledge him and he will make your paths straight!"* (Proverbs, Chapter 3 Verse 5). This is, in our view, perhaps the supreme way to gain the best direction for your life and to ensure the 'best is yet to come'.

2. Don't be limited by tradition, convention, environment, upbringing, or words that people have spoken over you. Decide to be all that you can be today and take the first step to achieve it.

3. Read books about people who have achieved great things, particularly when the 'odds were stacked

against them'. These days you can go on line and read about so many interesting people.

4. Get alongside people who will inspire you to greater things (and particularly to greater things in God). Learn from them; listen to their story, and how they arrived at where they are now. It will inspire you.

5. Keep learning! One of the characteristics of the people we have mentioned in this book is that they continued to learn, even as they went into 'midlife', and beyond.

6. Don't stop having goals, and aspirations for your life. The only person stopping you having them is you. Speak to yourself today, and believe that there is much you still need to achieve and can achieve.

7. Enjoy being on the adventure of a life time and don't see it as a routine, but as an exciting journey that will change you and others around you.

8. Start believing that you are going to be more productive, have more fun and more satisfying relationships with colleagues, family and friends.

Believe that you can have a stronger marriage and that you will be healthier, happier, and well on your way to a longer life. This kind of believing is medicine to the soul!

9. Recognise achievements in yourself and others, and regularly give praise and encouragement. Also gladly accept it yourself!

10. Celebrate life. Live life to the full. Never stop being thankful and give thanks in all circumstances! Never lose the 'fun child' in yourself and never stop being 'a refreshing person'.

Epilogue

Where Do We Go From Here?

(Eddie)

It is our hope that we have captured something of our heart and mission in life and shared some of the principles that we live by! The book was primarily written with mid-lifers in mind, but the more I have perused the pages I am convinced there is something in here for everyone! We hope that the principles in this book will help you in your life's journey, whether it be marriage, relationships, Church life, or in your career, no matter what stage of life you are at.

We began by suggesting to you that 'life is a journey' and it is so important to know where you are going. Our challenge is to determine what satellite navigation system we use for life, relationships, and for how we approach the subject of our Creator. It may be that you use a whole lot of common sense, but maybe something in these chapters will inspire you to 'look a little deeper'.

If you haven't seen the film 'Patch Adams' starring the very humorous Robin Williams then I would recommend it for your next viewing. He seems to capture, in such a down to earth and realistic way how important laughter really is, in a therapeutic sense, but also in everyday family and work life. I am told that we laugh a staggering three times less than we did in the 1950's. Remember, fundamentally, we don't need to be happy to laugh, but we can laugh to be happy. If laughter is the best medicine isn't it about time we all introduced it again to ever area of our everyday lives? Let's bring celebration back into ever moment of our lives!

Don't be pigeon holed by convention, or routines, but rather constantly allow yourself to be changed and renewed. It is a wonderful thing to see an 'older' person still young at heart and with a spirit of thankfulness in their life that causes them to reach out to other people with grace.

Let's step out of the stereotype of older people that are 'grumpy old men' or 'grumpy old women' and use our words to build people up. Let's not be cynical! Let's speak words of life! Remember, grumpy old people are grumpy young people who got old!

As a mid-lifer, don't have a 'midlife crisis' but be blessed with the way God had made you, and face life with confidence and faith for the future. Believe that the best is yet to come. There still is, within all of us, the ability and energy to be creative, to take risks, to do things we have never done, to visit new destinations, to learn a new language and to reach out and dream of greater things in our lives. You can do it! Start today and don't let age rob you of what you might become!

So mid-lifers you have a blank canvas in front of you right now. It's your choice what picture you paint and what colours you use! Why not make sure that the picture you paint is vibrant, exciting and attractive to those around you!

References

K. Blanchard & S. Johnson, The One Minute Manager (William Collins Sons & Co Ltd, 2000)

A. Ellis, The Essence Of RET (Journal of Rational Emotive Therapy, 1984)

D. Goleman, The New Leaders (Time Warner Books, 2002)

R. Holden, Laughter The Best Medicine (Harper Collins, 1993)

V. Oaklander, Windows To Our Children (Gestalt Journal Press, 1998)

E. Peterson, The Message (Nav Press Publishing Group, 1995)

K. H. Rodgers. Pearls Of Bizdom (Writersworld, 2006)

A. Sugar, The Apprentice (BBC Books, 2005)

J. & M. Tomlinson, The Luxury Of Time (Simon & Schuster, 2005)